LOSS OF A RELATIONSHIP

IN THIS
Devotions for
VERY
Your Time of Need
HOUR

JILL MARIE TAYLOR
& LAURA RODRIGUEZ

BROADMAN
& HOLMAN
PUBLISHERS

Nashville, Tennessee

Printed in the United States of America

4253-78
0-8054-5378-4

Dewey Decimal Classification: 242.4
Subject Heading:
DEVOTIONAL LITERATURE // HUMAN RELATIONS
Library of Congress Card Catalog Number: 94-4957

Unless noted otherwise, Scripture quotations are from the Holy Bible, *New International Version,* © 1973, 1978, 1984 by International Bible Society. Scriptures marked GNB are from the *Good News Bible,* the Bible in Today's English Version, © American Bible Society, Old Testament 1976 and New Testament 1966, 1971, 1976, used by permission; TLB from *The Living Bible,* © Tyndale House Publishers, Wheaton, Ill., 1971, used by permission; and RSV from the *Revised Standard Version of the Bible,* © 1946, 1952, 1971, 1973.

Library of Congress Cataloging-in-Publication Data
Taylor, Jill Marie, 1953–
   Devotions for your time of need. Loss of a relationship / by Jill Marie Taylor and Laura Rodriguez.
      p.   cm. — (In this very hour)
   ISBN 0-8054-5378-4
   1. Consolation. 2. Friendship—Religious aspects—Christianity—Prayer-books and devotions—English. 3. Loss (Psychology)—Religious aspects—Christianity—Prayer-books and devotions—English. I. Rodriguez, Laura.
II. Title. III. Series.
BV4909.T38   1994
  242'.4—dc20

94-4957
CIP

To my mother and grandfather,
who taught me the meaning of unconditional love.
To my son Patrick,
whom I comforted and was comforted by.
And to my husband Tim,
who encouraged me to write this book
so that others will know there is hope and healing
in any relationship.
Jill Marie Taylor

To my wonderful husband
and resident computer genius
whose humor brings healing to my soul.
To my selfless and sacrificing mother
who when I was a child went hungry
that I might eat.
To the world's three greatest children—
Pussycat, Curly-Bear, and Apatee.
With special acknowledgment to
Joshua Corel and his Kathy
who carry me through the battles.
Laura Rodriguez

Contents

PART ONE

JILL'S STORY

ℰ

HOW CAN THIS BE HAPPENING?

The day began much like any other. The dinner dishes were finished and our three-year-old daughter Emily was asleep. Giving nine-year-old Patrick a goodnight kiss, I sent him off to bed.

The house was quiet except for the TV program my husband Tim was watching. I disappeared into our bedroom to fold laundry. Later, Tim walked in, closing the door behind him.

"I need to talk to you," he said. His serious expression immediately told me there was something wrong, and my pulse quickened.

"I'm not happy in our marriage anymore," he said. "I've been talking to Jessie about a lot of things, and she's been caring and understanding. I've realized I'm in love with her."

His news shattered my once secure world. Jessie was our neighbor and my best friend. *How could this be happening?*

Numbed with pain, I listened as Tim rattled off a long list of grievances. Like a drowning woman, I grappled for a lifeline to save our relationship.

"Maybe we could try counseling," I sputtered.

Tim shook his head. "If we can't work out our own problems after seventeen years of marriage, then it's not worth working out." The rest of our conversation blurred into obscurity.

Over the next several days I tried to sort things out. Tim and I had known Jessie and her husband for years. Our children played together and we went out to dinner together; we had shared good times as well as bad. Jessie and I openly talked about our faith. Now I didn't understand how she could call herself a Christian or my friend while she accepted gifts, luncheon dates, time, and concern from my husband. I felt stupid and naive. After all, I was the one who asked Tim to hire Jessie as his bookkeeper when she was looking for a job. In trust and innocence, *I* had put the "other woman" right under his nose.

Little did I know at the time, that later she'd rely on Tim more and more as she went through a painful divorce. As they became emotionally involved, Tim turned to Jessie instead of discussing *our* problems with *me*. As their interest in each other increased, Jessie encouraged Tim to leave me. She told him that her divorce was the best thing she'd done and that he needed to do whatever it took to make him happy.

Somehow, however, Tim didn't leave me. We continued to drift apart as the weeks slipped into months. Even though Tim had refused counseling, I knew I couldn't get through this ordeal alone. I met with my pastor. It was good to have someone to lean on. But there was still no one to lean on or communicate with at home.

I longed to share this crisis with people who would understand, but my own relatives lived far away. Tim's family were the only relatives that were near us. Because Tim's parents worked with him, I knew Delores, his mother, was aware of the problem. Tim had told her how he felt about Jessie, yet his mother never approached me with concern or comfort. Not once did she say, "I love you and I don't want to see your family destroyed." She never asked how she could help us and never showed disapproval of Tim's actions.

Delores' betrayal ripped through my heart. But what hurt more was her continued companionship with Jessie. Why didn't she insist Jessie stay out of her son's life? Her actions told me that her friendship with "the other woman" was more valuable to her than the sanctity of her son's marriage or the importance of our relationship as "mother" and "daughter." It was then that I knew I couldn't trust her.

Since the two women worked together and socialized as well, I could no longer share with my mother-in-law any of my personal problems or feelings. Each day I was tormented, knowing that the three of them spent their working hours together. While their relationship grew, our marriage was being undermined. Emotionally alone and alienated from Tim's family, I worried. *How will this affect our children? Can we ever recapture the romance and friendship we had once enjoyed? Is our marriage over?*

Gone was the man I fell in love with and married. Tim had grown cold, indifferent, and unpredictable. He lost weight, grew a beard, and let his hair grow to his shoulders. We mechanically went through our day with little interaction. I did everything I could to prevent conflict. I guarded every word I said so we wouldn't fight. I didn't want to push him away—I wanted us to communicate so we'd have a chance to make our marriage work.

Over the next nine months, I sank into a deep depression. First, I lost my appetite for food. Then, I lost my appetite for living. After all this time, I was tired of trying my best. No matter what I did, it never seemed to be good enough. Tim continued in his same patterns; *he* didn't see anything wrong with his behavior.

I cried out to God, "Where are You? I can't go through this anymore. Tell me what to do, *please.*"

But when I couldn't hear His answers—when I began to seriously contemplate suicide—I realized I needed help. I talked to a friend who suggested I see a Christian counselor.

As I worked with the counselor, I saw the only way to truly love someone is through God. I had to decide to love Tim as God did, to regard him as a special creation God made and gave to me, and to serve God by showing Tim I loved him and not by trying to change him. Changing a heart is God's responsibility, not mine. It wasn't easy to do this and it didn't happen overnight. But soon I found my energy and confidence returning. I mustered the courage to go back to school. I updated my wardrobe, tried a new hairstyle, and got a job outside the home. My friends noticed the changes, and their comments encouraged me.

Tim noticed the changes too. Dinners spent in stony silence were now replaced with conversation. First, we talked about the weather and work. Then, with my confidence rising, I started telling some jokes—and he laughed! We were starting to communicate again. And although things were not perfect or back to normal, they were getting better.

℃

1

WHEN YOU'RE ANGRY

"In your anger do not sin." Do not let the sun
go down while you are still angry.

Ephesians 4:26–27

There were so many nights that I lay in bed, physically
and emotionally drained from the days' events. Hot,
angry tears would stream down my cheeks as I lay
alone in the dark.

I knew that sleep would bring much-needed rest.
But more than that, it offered the peaceful forgetful-
ness I longed for. It would provide a way to escape, to
lapse into unconsciousness and numb the pain that
had become my familiar companion.

However, sleep eluded me as my mind whirled. I
seethed with anger and hatred.

In the midst of all this conflict, I came across this
Bible passage. I felt relieved because it allowed me to
be human and to be angry. However, the passage also
said, "Do not let the sun go down while you are still
angry."

Each night I tried to release my anger to God so I
could sleep. Sometimes I succeeded, and sometimes
I didn't. You will be angry at the people who have hurt
you. But harboring this anger will hurt *you* more. Just
like me, you need rest. I pray that you "will lie down
and sleep in peace" (Ps. 4:8).

2

A Friend Indeed

If an enemy were insulting me, I could endure it; if a foe were raising himself against me, I could hide from him. But it is you, a man like myself, my companion, my close friend, with whom I once enjoyed sweet fellowship. . . .

But I call to God, and the LORD saves me. Evening, morning and noon I cry out in distress, and he hears my voice. He ransoms me unharmed from the battle waged against me, even though many oppose me.

Psalm 55:12–14, 16–18

How could my friend have so little regard for me? How could she intentionally hurt and betray me?

It's worse to be hurt by someone you're close to. I had invested love and time in our friendship. I trusted her and expected her to treat me with the same love and respect. This was the ultimate hurt. As a result, I was reluctant to establish new friendships. It was even harder to fully trust anyone because I was afraid they also would deceive me.

Through it all, however, there was one friendship I *could* count on—my friendship with the Lord. I trusted Him with dark secrets and deep pain, and He was always there. I had a true Friend in Jesus. You can call Him Friend, too. And He will never let you down.

3

WHEN YOU'RE AFRAID

God is our refuge and strength, an ever-present help in trouble. Therefore we will not fear, though the earth give way and the mountains fall into the heart of the sea, though its waters roar and foam and the mountains quake with their surging.

Psalm 46:1–3

My whole world was falling apart. I was so afraid. It was bad enough to find out Tim cared for another woman, but when he said he might move out, I began to worry. *What will happen to me and the children?* I wondered. Other than being a homemaker, I hadn't held a job in years.

Fear makes you feel so helpless. But when I looked in my Bible, I found comfort in Psalm 37:25: "I have never seen the righteous forsaken or their children begging bread."

Although throughout the uncertain days ahead anything could have happened, I was certain of one thing: that God would meet all my "needs according to his glorious riches in Christ Jesus" (Phil. 4:19). And He did.

Just as God was in control of my situation, He's in control of yours as well. No matter how bleak things look, God is bigger than your problems. Do not fear.

4

Jesus Understands

They went to a place called Gethsemane, and Jesus said to his disciples, "Sit here while I pray." He took Peter, James and John along with him, and he began to be deeply distressed and troubled. "My soul is overwhelmed with sorrow to the point of death, . . . Stay here and keep watch." . . . [When] he returned . . . [He] found them sleeping. . . . "Could you not keep watch for one hour?". . . Once more he went away. . . . When he came back, he again found them sleeping, because their eyes were heavy. . . . Returning the third time, he said to them, "Are you still sleeping and resting? Enough!"

Mark 14:32–34, 37, 39–41

When Jesus went to pray in the garden, He took His closest friends with Him. Facing betrayal, public humiliation, and death, He needed their support.

But upon returning, Jesus found them sleeping. In His great anguish, friends let Him down.

When you feel abandoned and alone, Jesus understands. He suffered the disappointment of betrayal by trusted friends, and the anger which resulted. He understands the pain of a broken heart. And He already knows what you are going through. Go ahead—you can trust Him. Tell Him how you feel.

5

LOVE ONE ANOTHER?

"You have heard that it was said, 'Love your neighbor and hate your enemy.' But I tell you: Love your enemies and pray for those who persecute you, that you may be sons of your Father in heaven."

Matthew 5:43–45

When I read the above verses, I laughed with bitter sarcasm at the commandment which seemed impossible for me to fulfill. Love my enemies. *Yeah, sure Lord. How can You expect me to love the people who are hurting me?*

Intellectually, I knew that I hated *what* they were doing, not them. But when you are hurting, it is difficult to look at the source of your pain intellectually. It is harder still to separate the behavior and the person.

Although I understood God's commandment to love one another, my excuse was that I'm human, not divine. I didn't know how to love my enemies and I didn't want to. I still have a hard time trying to love the people who hurt me.

Time has healed some wounds. I often wonder if I'll ever be able to freely love those who hurt me. But at least now I'm willing to try. Maybe that's the first step.

6

THE PROMISE OF A FUTURE

"For I know the plans I have for you," declares
the Lord, "plans to prosper you and not to harm
you, plans to give you hope and a future."

Jeremiah 29:11

One night my husband and I were quarreling in the
family room. Our son called out to me from his
bedroom. When I answered his frightened call, he
threw his arms around me, and sobbed into my
shoulder, "What's gonna happen to me?"

Swallowing hard, I struggled to hold back my own
tears. *How could I promise Patrick everything would be
all right when I had no idea what the future held for
us?* So I told him what I did know. No matter what
might happen between his father and me, we would
always love him.

Many times during that year I asked God that same
question, "What's going to happen to me, Lord?" Like
a little child, I too wanted promises that everything
was going to be all right.

I had to learn to live one day at a time and lean on
God's promises, even if the broken relationships in
my life were never restored. God has promised you
hope for tomorrow. No matter what you are going
through now, you can believe your generous and
loving Father has your future in His mighty hands.

7

LOSING A FRIEND

"For the Son of Man came to seek and to save what was lost."

Luke 19:10

"Mommy, why is Daddy acting so strange? I don't know who he is anymore."

When our son asked me these questions, I wanted to cry—not just for the loss of the beautiful relationship that had been between this father and our son, but for my loss too.

My husband was no longer the man I used to know. Gone was the best friend that I used to share *everything* with. After seventeen years of intimate companionship, I felt a loss that I thought no one would be able to replace. Would anybody else ever understand the real me? Would they even care?

In time, I did confide in a few close friends. My friends loved and accepted me, and our friendships gained new depth and trust.

My relationship with our son deepened also. We talked whenever he needed to. We often spoke about how much God loved us and how He'd see us through.

And as a beloved friend, the Lord was always there—seeking us and sustaining us. He's there for you, too.

8

BE STILL

"Be still, and know that I am God."
Psalm 46:10

When my husband first told me that he loved someone else, I found myself asking, "Why did this happen to *me*, Lord? Now what's going to happen? Will he leave me and our children? What should I do next?" I was afraid of what might happen and unsure of making any decisions.

I did pray during this time; however, I kept hearing the same thing over and over again—"Be still . . ." At first I was puzzled. How could I *be still* when so much was going on? My mind was filled with thoughts of anger, hatred, pity, and fear. My life was in constant turmoil, and I couldn't quiet the screaming voices inside me.

Months later I finally realized that God wants me to be at peace and trust Him no matter what I'm going through. It was only when I released my fears and asked God what *He* wanted me to do, that I clearly heard His message.

Listening to what others think you should do, or even trying to do everything yourself, will only get you into trouble. Be still and listen to God. After all, He knows your past, present, and future, and you can count on His direction.

9

WHEN YOUR LOSS AFFECTS OTHERS

Trust in the LORD with all your heart and lean
not on your own understanding; in all your ways
acknowledge him, and he will make your paths
straight.

Proverbs 3:5–6

When my husband's feelings for me changed, his
choices not only influenced our relationship but af-
fected other shared friendships as well.

His conduct in particular hurt a relationship
which our son and I enjoyed. A neighbor, an experi-
enced fisherman, had been teaching us his craft. One
day, however, his wife called me and said she'd no
longer allow her husband to take us fishing while my
marriage was so shaky.

I was angry. We were robbed of a favorite hobby
because of my husband's irresponsible behavior. Why
did his actions have to reflect on me and ruin the
friendship with our neighbor in the process? After all,
he was the one who had changed, not me.

That's when I came across the above Scripture and
discovered how heavily I'd been leaning on my own
understanding. I had to choose to rely on God, and
not myself, for the solutions to my pain.

You can trust Him, too. Even though you don't
understand the terrible things happening in your life

right now, be assured that God will straighten out any rough road you find yourself on, if you put your confidence in Him.

10

DON'T GIVE UP!

Let us keep our eyes fixed on Jesus, on whom our faith depends from beginning to end. He did not give up because of the cross! . . .Think of what he went through; how he put up with so much hatred from sinful men! So do not let yourselves become discouraged and give up.

Hebrews 12:2–3, GNB

I wanted to give up. In solitude I'd scream, "Enough is enough, Lord! I can't handle this anymore!" I was tired of fighting, trying, hoping, and crying. I didn't want to face another day or another problem.

God understood, and out of a casual acquaintance He brought forth a good friend who gave this advice: "I can't tell you what to do, and I can't take your problems away. But I can tell you to keep your eyes fixed on the cross. Don't give up—no matter what."

Her words were a lifeline to me. In the midst of chaos, there was a constant—my Lord and Savior. I pray that you, too, will remember that Jesus is your closest friend. Your friendship with Him will *never* end. So don't give up.

11

WHEN YOU'RE BETRAYED

Even my close friend, whom I trusted, he who
shared my bread, has lifted up his heel against
me. But you, O LORD, have mercy on me . . .

Psalm 41:9–10

She had been my friend for years. As next door neighbors we spoke often, sharing dreams, secrets, joys,
and failures. It devastated me when I discovered we
also shared my husband.

When I realized what was happening, I felt de-
ceived. I'd never suspected a thing.

Betrayed, I cried out to the Lord. "How could You
have let this happen to me? I trusted them—I trusted
You. Now what do I do?"

God's answer was clear. He reminded me when
Jesus was betrayed by Judas. Even though Jesus was
deeply grieved by what His disciple—His friend—
had done, He still loved him and was ready to forgive.

This concept was almost impossible for me to
grasp and even more absurd to think about doing.
"Why should I do this?" I asked God. "After all, they
betrayed me." But the truth is that God loves the
people who hurt me as much as He loves me.

Knowing I had to obey God's command that we
"love one another," I eventually was able to confess
my unwillingness to forgive, and then ask God to help

me to forgive those who had hurt me. It didn't change their actions, but it changed me.

I pray you too will begin the process of forgiveness—for your sake as well as for those who may have hurt you.

12

HAVE THINE OWN WAY, LORD

"Woe to him who quarrels with his Maker, to him who is but a potsherd among the potsherds on the ground. Does the clay say to the potter, 'What are you making?'"

Isaiah 45:9

There were times when I hurt so badly that I couldn't do much of anything. I didn't want to talk or cry or pray. I wanted to be left alone, but that only reminded me of how lonely I felt without the friendships that had meant so much to me.

I often sang the old hymn "Have Thine Own Way, Lord"—softly, meaningfully, and finally, tearfully. By opening the floodgates of my soul, I let God in—to hold me, to heal me, and to have His own way.

Don't be afraid to try different ways to open your heart and soul to God so that He can minister to you. Do whatever it takes—pray, sing, meditate, or write your feelings in a journal. You may even need to scream or cry. That's okay. There is no set formula that works the same for everyone. Just take the first step and God will meet you there.

13

You're a Valuable Person

"Are not two sparrows sold for a penny? Yet not one of them will fall to the ground apart from the will of *your* Father. And even the very hairs of your head are all numbered. So don't be afraid; you are worth more than many sparrows."

Matthew 10:29–31

In the midst of our troubled relationship—and armed with a list of accusations—my husband blamed me for our problems. He also said that our friends and *my* family felt the same way.

His words wounded me; I felt worthless. Although I knew that any relationship requires give and take on both sides, I wondered if I really were to blame.

I discussed the matter with my family and friends. They revealed they'd never said the things he claimed. Discovering the facts freed me to regain my self-confidence. I was willing to acknowledge my failures and make changes, but I wouldn't accept all the responsibility for our damaged relationship. If someone has told you you're worthless, don't believe them. It's a lie. The truth is God loves you so much that He allowed His only Son, to die on the cross so *you* could have eternal life. You are valuable and you are loved!

14

THIS IS A DAY OF NEW BEGINNINGS

This is a day of new beginnings,
time to remember and move on,
time to believe what love is bringing,
laying to rest the pain that's gone.

Then let us, with the Spirit's daring,
step from the past and leave behind
our disappointment, guilt, and grieving,
seeking new paths, and sure to find.

Christ is alive, and goes before us
to show and share what love can do.
This is a day of new beginnings,
our God is making all things new.

—*Hymn by Brian Wren**

Two years ago as I sang this hymn in church, I began realized that I had never let go of the past hurts. Neither had I completely forgiven each of the people involved. Without doing that, I couldn't "move on."

I've learned that forgiveness is a process. Anger kept me from forgiving the people who'd hurt me.

After a time, I found that I really *wanted* to forgive those who had hurt me. But sometimes—with no warning at all—the memories would flood into my mind, and the pain would return, as fresh as ever.

This made me wonder if I'd ever *really* forgiven them at all. Then I remembered that Jesus said we should forgive "seventy times seven" (Matt. 18:22, RSV). This means I'm to forgive over and over again.

The next time I felt the pain begin to rise up within me, I decided to make a conscious choice to forgive. This was the only way I was able to completely let go of it and give it back to God for Him to deal with. It took four years before I could let go and move on.

If your loss is recent, you may not be ready to let go and forgive. Healing takes time, and each step is important. Know that God is there to guide you through this process. He's asking you to forgive and move on to a new beginning.

15

TO TRUST AGAIN

When I am afraid, I will trust in you. In God, whose word I praise, in God I trust; I will not be afraid. What can mortal man do to me?

Psalm 56:3–4

"What can mortal man do to me?" I screamed out to God during my morning devotions. "You've got to be kidding! This 'mortal woman' has ruined my life and marriage by her deception, and now my own husband is a liar—I'll never trust anyone again." Betrayed, I also wondered if I could trust God. After all, wasn't He the One who let this happen?

It took time to realize that God was aware of my situation and had plans to restore my marriage. I discovered that when I trust God and do what His Word says, God will see me through the hard times.

Although my husband never said he was sorry, I got something better—repentance. He turned away from the other woman, changed his old ways, and started a new life with me. It's taken a few years to rebuild complete trust in him, but I'm glad I gave him a second chance and let God repair our relationship.

God is bigger than any problem a mere mortal can throw your way. Trust Him to help you find solutions. And then give Him time to work it out.

16

There Is Hope

Now glory be to God who by his mighty power at work within us is able to do far more than we would ever dare to ask or even dream of—infinitely beyond our highest prayers, desires, thoughts, or hopes.

Ephesians 3:20, TLB

"When will this get better, Lord?" I asked, half expecting an audible answer. Although I prayed for reconciliation, nothing positive seemed to happen in my marriage. As each day dragged into another, I lost hope.

There were times I didn't know why I bothered to pray. Then God answered me with the above Scripture. I'd been asking for a good marriage, but now I dared to ask for a relationship better than I could dream of.

God has given me that marriage. Making changes in our relationship wasn't easy, but after five years, it *has* happened! We now have a great marriage—not perfect—but far better than what I originally asked God for.

Life isn't easy. But remember what Jesus said: "In this world you will have trouble. But take heart! I have overcome the world" (John 16:33). Knowing I have Christ gives me the ability to persevere during troubling times. And He's there for you too.

ℭ

PART TWO

LAURA'S STORY

$\mathscr{C}$

A FATHER'S LOVE

Done with the funeral arrangements, my husband Sam and I entered my father's mobile home and collapsed at the table. Outside, Florida oaks swayed in a rainy wind. The weather seemed to mimic my mood as I recalled the events leading to my father's death.

Two nights before, worlds away in our Pennsylvania home, Sam and I were awakened by a phone call from a young woman who'd been seeing my father. The syrupy concern in her voice sounded rehearsed. She said, "Your father's had a heart attack. He's been rushed to the hospital. It doesn't look good."

I felt my neck muscles tense and my pulse quicken. Arrangements were made for us to go to Daytona Beach and for Mother, long divorced from my father, to look after our teenage children. Rubbing my aching temples, I prayed constantly, "Lord, heal my father. Comfort him."

Before Sam and I touched down in Florida, however, my father passed away. Then later the cruel reality struck again. A letter from my father's insurance company said the beneficiary of his meager policy had been changed from me to his girlfriend. Wondering if my own father had rejected me on his deathbed, I sobbed aloud and fell into Sam's arms. Had I not only lost my father but his heart as well? Following my nightmarish, abuse-ridden childhood, that was a treasure I'd only recently gained.

As long as I can remember, my father's rejection has haunted me. This probably began when he abandoned his wife and infant son for the teenage girlfriend who said, "It's either your wife or me!" That girlfriend would soon give birth to me.

Forever discarding his former family, my father began divorce proceedings. Although he married my mother, he also began to resent her for her ultimatum. When I was born, that resentment passed to me. Later, that resentment grew into physical abuse which included beatings and starvation for both my mother and me. Following their short, violent marriage my parents, mercifully, divorced.

But that was long ago. I thought my father and I had made amends. But now, he was rejecting me from the grave. I could only weep, "Oh God! Oh God!"

I wanted to hate my father, but I couldn't. Instead, I hated his girlfriend.

And so from Pennsylvania, Sam and I participated in a painful, legal battle. Her court deposition stated that my father had preferred her to me as a daughter and that I "didn't care much for him."

"Lies! All lies," I'd cry.

Still, a sixty-forty compromise in her favor divided my father's policy. To me, that was a slap in the face that only sharpened the agony of having my father reject me for another. I felt orphaned. By allowing this to happen, even God seemed to have turned His face from me. My prayers became foggy and difficult, my emotions explosive. Venting my anger on Sam, I spoke hatefully to him. In turn, he withdrew into the comfortable numbness of the television. Sometimes, I'd goad him too far and he'd boomerang my anger back to me. From all this, our children escaped into various teenage mischiefs. Before long, spiritual and emotional distress translated to physical. My already lean frame dropped an additional thirty pounds, and I picked up one virus after another. Prolonging my agony, Sam and I couldn't settle my father's estate. The court ruled that before probate could begin, my father's long-lost son, Allen, must be located and given an opportunity to contest the will.

Despite my struggles, the court's edict rekindled in me a long suppressed yearning to meet my brother. A Bible verse convinced me that God would bring this about: "Delight yourself in the LORD and he will give you the desires of your heart" (Ps. 37:4).

Perhaps through Allen, I thought, *a part of my relationship with my father could be redeemed.* I began to search for him.

But when years passed without a clue, I began to doubt the promise God had given. While reading a magazine in a doctor's office, however, Sam learned that the Social Security Administration would locate missing persons for estate purposes. Immediately we contacted them. Within days Allen was found and gave permission for me to have his phone number.

A few days before Christmas, I trembled while dialing his number. A harsh sounding woman answered the phone. Though intimidated by her tone, I identified myself and the purpose of my call. Nothing could have prepared me for her response.

"I'm Allen's mother," the woman roared. "So you're that tramp's dirty little brat!"

A gut reaction of harsh words nearly exploded from my mouth. However, wanting to speak with Allen, I bit them back. Finally, he came to the phone.

I tried to sound cheerful. But from the beginning, Allen sounded disinterested. Both he and his mother made it obvious they'd never forgiven my father for abandoning them. Once Allen learned that our father had died penniless and that probate was merely a legal formality, his disinterest turned to coldness.

When I called him again on Christmas day, he said he had no desire to contest our father's will. Another message came through loud and clear: Neither did he have any desire to pursue his relationship with me.

Although Allen had never known our father, I realized he'd joined him in rejecting me. My emotions numbed. Through my tears, the lights of our Christmas tree melted into a colorful haze. Beneath it, however, a small wooden manger shone through. Inside, a baby Jesus in a cradle made me remember the true meaning of Christmas—which is God born to die to bring people forgiveness. Cradle to cross—neither life nor death were easy for Jesus. He was born in a barn, worked as a carpenter, and at only thirty-three suffered the agony of crucifixion. But He chose Calvary's difficult path for every person created.

Gazing at the manger beneath my Christmas tree, I stood before another difficult path. Either I could choose it and forgive my father and all the others for hurting me, or I could go the way of anger and revenge. In raw obedience to God, I turned my back on vengeance and chose to walk the path of forgiveness. I knew this would not be easy, nor would it be short. However, at this path's end, I saw not a manger, but a mansion.

17

Our Loving Father

For we do not have a high priest who is unable
to sympathize with our weaknesses.

Hebrews 4:15

For the longest time I found it difficult to call God,
Father. Jesus, Holy Spirit, Bridegroom—all those
came easily to my mind and prayers, but not *Father*.
Calling God by that name evoked only frightening
images of God with my earthly father's face—and
disposition.

If I stepped the slightest bit out of line, would God
slap me suddenly like my father did? My father also
disinherited and disowned me. Would God?

One day I heard a Christian say something that
helped explain my feelings: "A person's perception of
God is influenced by his or her natural father." *That's
true*, I thought. Even as a Christian, I attached my
father's personality to God. I lived in fear that my
slightest mistake would send Him into a violent rage.

Then Scriptures like the one above convinced me
that God knows that I see Him as I do because I've
been hurt. His hands don't reach to slap; they reach
to embrace.

Slowly, I am realizing that God is a kind Father who
wants only the best for my life. And now I am finding
it easier to call God *Father*.

18

GOD LOVES YOU

"I have loved you with an everlasting love."
Jeremiah 31:3

After my father died, a heartbreaking realization struck: I can't remember him ever telling me he loved me or displaying any love.

Throughout childhood, I ached for masculine affection. That ache continued until my husband came along and soothed the pain with the tonic of human love. But human love is not perfect and tonic wears off. With the tension surrounding my father's death, that tonic wore off in a cruel way—my husband and I started to bicker. The comfort he had provided seemed to fly right out the window.

In desperation, I turned to the Scriptures. I discovered a passionate God who never tires of expressing His love. His words are not a temporary tonic. They are eternal "streams of living water" (John 7:38).

To you and me, He says, "I have loved you with an everlasting love; . . . I have summoned you by name; you are mine. . . . I have engraved you on the palms of my hands"(Isa. 43:1; 49:16).

His words give us life: He *loves* us. In response, can you declare your love to Him?

If people, created in the image of God, crave love, then He must also. And yours is the love He craves.

19

God's Faithfulness

"And surely I am with you always, to the very end of the age."

Matthew 28:20

Following my father's death, Sam and I remained in Florida several days. During that time, we hired a lawyer to contest the change of beneficiary in my father's insurance policy. In his office, I let Sam do the talking. All I could do was sit and stare with tear-glazed eyes that poorly veiled my emotions. *How could my own father have rejected me for another?*

Back at his house we noticed that many expensive items were missing. Neighbors informed us that they'd seen his girlfriend loading things into a pickup truck under the cover of darkness.

I wanted to scream at the injustice of it all. *Where was God in my misery?*

Bit by bit, He answered my question with a simple, yet profound truth. He was with me. She may have stolen my father's possessions and even his heart, but no one could steal God or His commitment to be with me always.

Today, no matter who or what's been stolen from you, remember God's presence and love are secure. Forever, His heart is sealed to yours. No one can tear it away.

20

A Ticking Time Bomb

See to it that no one misses the grace of God and that no bitter root grows up to cause trouble and defile many.

Hebrews 12:15

The illness struck suddenly, jolting me awake at night with cold sweats and stabbing chills. Soon, a deathlike cold turned my fingers into icy prongs that shocked whomever they touched. A frightening weakness settled in my heart. Beneath the skin stretched over my ribs, it could be seen racing, then pausing. All the while, it ached with hatred—my father, his girlfriend, even for my husband who didn't seem to understand.

This verse warns that bitterness and hatred can trouble and defile. My deteriorated health bears witness to that truth. Today, doctors have finally caught on to what God always knew. Within the human body, unresolved anger is a ticking time bomb.

No matter who hurts you or how, hate accomplishes nothing. I nearly ruined my health and marriage—I wound up worse than those I wasted my energies hating.

If you feel bitter toward someone, do what I know I must to survive: Commit your offenders and their offenses to God and never take them back. Only then can healing begin.

21

The Road of Humiliation

> I offered my back to those who beat me, my cheeks to those who pulled out my beard; I did not hide my face from mocking and spitting.
>
> *Isaiah 50:6*

One misty autumn day, I stood outside with my friend, bemoaning the fact that my father's girlfriend had humiliated me. Her expression serious, she listened. I'd wanted her sympathy, but instead, she made a statement that chilled my spirit: "Sometimes God allows His people to be embarrassed."

Later, while walking home, I felt offended and misunderstood. It took a long time for me to realize that what my friend said, though perhaps ill-timed, was true.

God could have stopped anything that happened anytime He wanted, yet He allowed me to be embarrassed. Eventually, I realized that this is something He also allowed for Himself. The Scriptures teach that Jesus was whipped, spat upon, stripped of His clothing, and crucified with criminals.

If rejection by another has embarrassed you, take comfort that God has traveled the road of humiliation. It's called Calvary.

That's where God lifted my shame from me. He removed *your* shame there also.

22

DADDY'S OPEN ARMS

And by him we cry, "Abba, Father."
Romans 8:15

Throughout my childhood I longed for a daddy like my friends had—a daddy whose touch was gentle, whose words were kind and whose arms were welcoming. My daddy's touch was often brutal, his words harsh, and his arms rejecting.

Into adulthood and even after my conversion to Christianity, deep childhood needs remained unfulfilled. A part of my soul felt like an empty room where a daddy belonged, but never really was. When my father died, all hopes of ever filling that room died too. I closed its door.

However, as I read Bible verses about God as Father, the door to that room cracked slowly open. Outside, my child's soul peeked through the crack.

From the room, dancing firelight poured out to warm my skin. Inside, I saw a large fireplace with its crackling blaze, and before it, a rocking chair atop a woven rug. Sitting in the chair, was a strongly built, but tender-expressioned Man.

Slowly, the great figure turned to greet me with a dazzling smile and extended arms. My heart pounded as I recognized God and mouthed the words, "Abba, Father."

Still, the question remains, will I run into His open arms? Will you? Faith's door is open and the Father longs for your fellowship. Rush to Him. Trust Him. Pour out your heart. Only He can fill the empty rooms of your soul.

23

HIS UNCONDITIONAL LOVE

Therefore, there is now no condemnation for those who are in Christ Jesus.

Romans 8:1

He who was seated on the throne said, "I am making everything new!"

Revelation 21:5

As a child, it devastated me to find a lump of coal in my Christmas stocking. Decades later, I still recall the condemnation I felt at having my behavior so harshly judged by my parents.

Similar emotions resurfaced when my father died rejecting me. After all, there was a grain of truth to his girlfriend's accusations—I *had* neglected him. The responsibilities of raising a family had preoccupied my thoughts. My father's rejection made me wonder if God was giving me another lump of coal.

Are there any coals in your life, any relationships in which you feel condemned? If so, take comfort in what I learned. Our Heavenly Father doesn't keep a coal bucket. Neither does He expect us to fully meet or understand the needs of another. Only He can satisfy the human heart. Best of all, nothing we can do—or not do—makes Him love us less.

The Bible tells us that God is "making everything new." To me, that means He hasn't forgotten broken relationships. One wonderful day, He'll hand us those lumps of coal transformed into glittering diamonds.

24

THE SHEPHERD'S HEART

He tends his flock like a shepherd: He gathers the lambs in his arms and carries them close to his heart.

Isaiah 40:11

Has someone you loved closed their arms and heart to you, like my father did to me? Do you find yourself wandering like a lost sheep, craving affection? I did.

In the Bible, Jesus is called "the good shepherd" (John 10:11). One day, His great love drove Him to search out this lonely little sheep. When He found me, I accepted Him into my heart and was born again. As He drew me to His bosom, I found a place reserved only for me. Near that secure place I discovered many other contented lambs, all with places of their own. If you're a Christian, you are one of them. If not, the

Shepherd's arms are reaching out to gather you in. There's always room for one more.

When human arms and hearts close and turn away, it's reassuring to know that the Shepherd's never will. And when His little lambs hurt, He embraces us tighter. Snuggle in close. Listen for His heart. It's beating with love for you.

25

LOVE'S GOLDEN DOOR

Your love, O LORD, reaches to the heavens, your faithfulness to the skies.

Psalm 36:5

As my father lay dying, one question rang in my mind, *Is my father a Christian?*

Gazing out the airplane window into dark, rolling clouds, I recalled he'd once made a profession of faith. When debt and illness struck, however, he'd blamed God and turned away.

Over and over I prayed, *Lord, please give both my father and me peace about his salvation!*

Suddenly, the dark clouds parted, revealing a golden opening similar to a door. From within, brilliant shafts of light danced to the earth. As Sam and I watched in awe, we said the shafts of light looked like tunnels to heaven. Meanwhile, something prompted us to notice the time the panorama faded—2:10 P.M.

Arriving at the airport, we called the hospital to check on my father's condition. A nurse told us he had passed away an hour before— 2:10 P.M.

As I burst into tears, Sam and I exchanged astonished glances. We both realized that though my father had let go of God, God had never let go of him.

Today, no matter how insecure and out of control life may feel, remember, God is also holding on if you belong to Him. Though others may let go, He never, never will. His love will carry you through this present crisis, and one day through love's golden door.

26

THE HANGMAN'S TREE

"Father, forgive them, for they do not know what they are doing."

Luke 23:34

As facts about my father's girlfriend were uncovered, I longed for the vigilante justice of the Old West. Back then, a lynch mob would ride after her into the wilderness, and then hang her from the highest tree. I wanted her to pay for her crimes, but she didn't. She'd tricked the justice system with her lies.

Pictures of the lynch mob and hangman's tree remained in my mind, however. During one prayer time, though, I remembered another mob and another tree. This mob screamed, "Crucify him! Crucify him!" But He who hung on the tree prayed for those who would hurt and kill Him. "Father, forgive them, for they do not know what they are doing."

A shocking prompting by the Holy Spirit urged me to do the same. Everything in me rebelled at the thought, but I obeyed, *"Father, forgive her . . ."*

Complete forgiveness came with far more time and difficulty. Still, that day, I realized something that changed my outlook: On Calvary's "hangman's tree," God had taken not only my place, but hers too.

For your own peace of mind, pray for those who've hurt you. God loves them too.

27

THE GOOD SAMARITAN

A man was going down from Jerusalem to Jericho, when he fell into the hands of robbers. They stripped him of his clothes, beat him and went away, leaving him half dead. . . . But a Samaritan, as he traveled, came where the man was; and when he saw him, he took pity on him. He went to him and bandaged his wounds, pouring on oil and wine.

Luke 10:30, 33–34

When our family moved to Florida, the wounds I'd received had left my emotions bleeding. Spiritually and physically sick, I drifted through several churches. I finally found one where the minister of counseling took me under his wing and poured the oil and wine of the Holy Spirit on my wounds.

He assured me that no matter who has rejected me, God never would. He told me the anger I'd been feeling toward my husband was something called transference: I'd been working out my hostilities toward my father on him. Knowing these facts and many others helped to release healing in me. Godly counseling can do the same for you.

If rejection has left you wounded and bleeding, pray for at least one good Samaritan to confide in. Through that person, receive God's healing. When you're ready, pass it along. Be a good Samaritan and help bandage the wounds of another.

28

A Father's Legacy

"The LORD, the LORD, the compassionate and gracious God, slow to anger, abounding in love and faithfulness, maintaining love to thousands, and forgiving wickedness, rebellion and sin. Yet he does not leave the guilty unpunished; he punishes the children and their children for the sin of the fathers to the third and fourth generation."

Exodus 34:6–7

My brother's unwillingness to meet me multiplied the sorrow inflicted by our father. I couldn't understand why someone wouldn't be curious to know their own flesh and blood.

I realized Allen's mother hated my father and programmed their son to do the same. For over forty years, Allen's anger had been stockpiling like dynamite. When I called, it exploded! I'd stood in as an emotional bombing range for our dead father.

Long ago I heard a wise minister say, "If you hate someone long enough, you'll end up just like them." Recognizing my father's tendencies in myself, I don't want to pass them to my children. Only forgiveness can stop this cycle. But forgiveness is not an emotion. It is a surrender of vengeance, and a process.

If harboring hatred makes us hateful, could then forgiveness and love make us more like He who *is* love? The legacy we pass to our children is up to us.

Oh, God, Ultimate Forgiver of all, as You forgave me on Calvary, help me to also forgive others.

29

THE FATHER'S HOUSE

"Do not let your hearts be troubled. Trust in God; trust also in me. In my Father's house are many rooms."

John 14:1–2

My earthly father's house was a rundown mobile home in Florida where our family traveled for special occasions like Christmas. Because I'm from the north, twinkling lights and Christmas carols never felt right among palm trees and sunny beaches—and neither did my relationship with my father. From my childhood, unresolved conflicts dimmed the holiday's glow.

Have any relational doors closed in disappointment for you? If so, take hope that one day a door of joy and fulfillment promises to open. And it opens to the Father's palace into which you will be escorted by angels. Inside, the Father will replace your disappointment with satisfaction, questions with answers, and tears with laughter.

Picture yourself at the Father's banquet table celebrating an eternal Christmas no conflict can overshadow. Feel His hand tenderly caress your cheek while He whispers, "You are precious and honored in my sight (Isa. 43:4), . . . [You are] the apple of my eye" (Zech. 2:8).

30

THE NASTY NOW AND NOW

And we know that in all things God works for the good of those who love him.

Romans 8:28

When my father died rejecting me, by faith I knew that good would ultimately result. However, that was in the "sweet by and by." I needed to see some good in "the nasty now and now," as my pastor calls it.

At the time of his death, my father owed for several months of mortgage debt. I was unable to repay, the bank threatened to repossess his mobile home and lot.

It looked like that would happen until Sam suddenly remembered his older brother, Danny, had long dreamed of retiring to Florida. Immediately we called him, offering the property in exchange for his payment of my father's debt. Excitedly agreeing, Danny left for Florida the next day.

Before long, Sam and Danny learned that months before my father's death, their elderly mother had begun praying for Danny to receive a place in Florida. Hearing this was a ray of light in an otherwise dark situation. Despite all the wrong surrounding my father's death, at least God had worked some of it for good, right here in the "nasty now and now"!

Look for good to come from your situation as well.

31

PAID IN FULL

"I will repay you for the years the locusts have eaten."

Joel 2:25

The locust had eaten many things that should have been mine. By far the most painful was my relationship with my father. The locust had also decimated my inheritance. Likewise consumed was the chance I'd ever meet my brother. My health and my relationship with my husband were also missing pieces.

Enemy forces, it seemed, were gnawing at me. I wondered, *What will be left when they finish?*

Does this describe the way you feel? If so, take comfort. God will repay us for our sufferings. The loss of my father's affections was repaid with a more intimate relationship with Father God, who is repaying my stolen inheritance with "treasures in heaven, where moth and rust do not destroy, and where thieves do not break in and steal" (Matt. 6:20).

The unfulfilled relationship with my brother was fulfilled with spiritual brothers and sisters within the family of God. As God imparts wisdom concerning my physical and spiritual rest, vitamins, and also forgiveness, my health is improving. And as my husband and I learn to treat each other as we would want to be treated, so is our marriage.

One by one, God is destroying the locusts that tried to destroy me. Stand back and watch Him fight for you!

C

EPILOGUE

FORGIVENESS IS THE KEY

It's been years since Jill and I suffered the pain of our broken relationships. During that time, people offered the old adage, "Time heals all wounds." But we've found that statement incomplete. The essential ingredient in the healing process is forgiveness.

At first, what had happened to us made us burn with anger—toward the ones who had hurt us, our circumstances, and, yes, even toward God.

We needed to acknowledge that anger. But dealing with the anger was only the first step of our individual journeys toward forgiveness.

Because God urges us to cast all our anxiety on Him, (see 1 Pet. 5:7) He isn't shocked by our gut-level emotions. That's called intimacy. And God longs for intimacy with His people. Scream, cry, do whatever you must. But don't hold your anger inside. It's a potential time bomb which can seriously damage your health.

God loves us, but He also loves those who have hurt us. The Scriptures say, God "is kind to the ungrateful and wicked" (Luke 6:35), and that He "wants all men to be saved" (1 Tim. 2:4).

We finally recognized that God wants us to forgive "seventy times seven" (Matt. 18:22, RSV). And if God wants to forgive our enemies, who are we not to do likewise?

We took to heart what we knew in our heads. As the righteous Judge, only God is worthy of measuring out punishment. The Word says, "All have sinned and fall short of the glory of God" (Rom. 3:23). But God loved us so much He sent Jesus (see John 3:16). On Calvary's cross, Jesus took upon Himself the punishment deserved by us all. Those of us who have accepted His atoning sacrifice call ourselves Christians. Since we have received God's mercy, He desires that we reflect that mercy to an unbelieving world. Through us, God can draw people to Him.

Our walk often takes us along a dark and rocky road. On this road, we cling to God and trust in His Word. Both will guide us into ever-increasing light. Just as a walk has a beginning, it also has an end—when God completes the good work He's started in us (see Phil. 1:6). Part of the good work He is accomplishing in us is our anger transforming to mercy.

Both of us have vowed at one time or another to "never forget." Maybe you have too. If God would only allow us to forget, it would be so much easier to forgive. But God leaves our memories intact so we can use them to help others.

Jesus taught us to pray,

"Dear Father God, 'Forgive us our sins, just as we have forgiven those who have sinned against us'" (Matt. 6:12, TLB).

For eternity's sake, for your own sake, pray and mean this prayer in your heart—and then act in obedience to it. In time, your feelings will catch up to you. Ours did.

May God bless you as you recover from your loss.